"Can prayer really be taught? Is it just the gift that some spiritual giants somehow have? This book by Wezeman and Fournier gives the kind of practical, yet imaginatively spiritual help to move into exploring one's conversation with God. I suspect that many of us who are no longer technically 'children' have much to learn from it.

"Wezeman and Fournier deliver what the title promises—20 prayer lessons for children. But so much is not said in the title. The lessons are practical and yet imaginative. I think it would be great fun to go through these lessons. If you are not a 'teacher,' then borrow some children (perhaps grandchildren on a visit or godchildren) and join them in learning exciting things about prayer."

Dr. Loren B. Mead
Founder, The Alban Institute
Washington, DC

"From the overview to the conclusion, the reader's attention is caught by these innovative prayer experiences for children. The clarity and conciseness of the format allow everyone to enhance their prayer experiences. The authors' use of the alliterative Goal-Gather-Guide is a wonderful tool. This consistency throughout the book allows you, as prayer facilitator, to prepare an unforgettable experience. The children focus on the prayer and are not distracted by the unexpected.

"The materials help students become better acquainted with God through traditional prayer and the Bible. The required materials are readily available and easy to use, even for the artistically challenged.

"The book provides a unique means of prayer for children. It assists them with the expression of prayer through word and art."

Sr. Marie Bernadette
Mrs. Deborah Ann Crimi
Catholic Grade School Teachers
Ridgewood, NY

"Phyllis Wezeman and Jude Fournier give us practical, hands-on activities to use with children and young people in congregations and homes. In *20 Prayer Lessons for Children*, they furnish teachers, parents, and worship leaders with choices for experiential learning in the area of prayer.

"Prayer is vital to the Christian life, something that is best learned through actual doing. Wezeman and Fournier have created imaginative ways to enhance the "learning to pray" process. In clear, concise language, they lay out the goals, needed materials, and explanations for carrying out twenty lessons that use the numbers one to twenty as the organizing points."

Helene G. Zwyghuizen
Consultant, Children in Worship
Author, *Leading Children in Worship*

"This book is a gift to any teacher preparing to tell the Good News! It serves as a valuable resource book. Traditional theology is presented in a contemporary fashion, scripture plays a central role in each chapter, and the subject matter can be easily adapted to children of a variety of age levels and still keep the heart of the lesson. The materials listed for each chapter are simple and easy to prepare.

"An invitation to prayer, an opportunity to pray, a realization that prayer can be a part of our daily experience—this is what Phyllis and Jude offer us."

Sr. Luke Dworschak, O.P.
Oakhurst, NJ

"This book is for all of us who have ever planned *one* lesson on prayer for children and then moved on to the next topic. The authors call us back to count the ways that prayer moves through our Christian faith and life. They invite us to experience the communion of saints across time and in our time. They use Scripture for instruction and inspiration. And, as this creative team has done before on other projects, they teach children to pray with all of the senses, with the mind and heart, with the resources of the church, and with every way in which we live and move and have our being."

Rev. Stephen C. Koldercup
Associate Pastor, First Presbyterian Church
Elkhart, IN

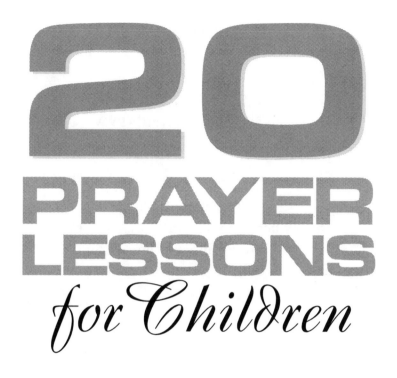

20 PRAYER LESSONS for Children

PHYLLIS VOS WEZEMAN
JUDE DENNIS FOURNIER

TWENTY-THIRD PUBLICATIONS
Mystic, CT 06355

Dedication

To Sr. Elaine DesRosiers,
an answer to prayer! (PVW)

To Valerie Keller,
for her commitment to the Gospel,
her care for life and humankind,
and most especially, for her friendship to me. (JDF)

Second printing 1997

Twenty-Third Publications
185 Willow Street
P.O. Box 180
Mystic, CT 06355
(860) 536-2611
800-321-0411

ISBN 0-89622-689-1
Library of Congress Catalog Card Number 95-62294
Printed in the U.S.A.

Table of Contents

Overview

Prayer is _____. Fill in the blank. This timeless, yet timely, statement has been pondered by teachers and students throughout the ages. And, this seemingly simple statement has been completed with answers ranging from a single word to multiple volumes.

Webster defines prayer as "the act of praying; an entreaty, supplication; a humble request, as to God; any set formula for this." Commentators and theologians call prayer communicating with God, opening one's life to God, engaging oneself in the purposes of God, and total immersion in the holy presence of God.

Prayer is a vital part of the Christian life, and we learn about prayer in many ways. By turning to Scripture, we discover how people in the Old Testament and the New Testament talked with and listened to God. We glean insight into prayer by reading stories of the saints, and we gain instruction about prayer from people of faith today. Perhaps our best guide to learning what prayer is, however, is to actually pray. And that's what this book provides—twenty prayer opportunities, appropriate for classroom or group use, designed to help participants explore and experience various aspects of and approaches to prayer.

Instruction takes place through involvement as participants explore and experience inviting, informing, inspiring activities that are used to impart information and ideas. As a unique feature and a fresh approach, each lesson involves a number, from one to twenty, that becomes the focus for the prayer experience.

Methods used to teach the subject matter incorporate architecture, art, banners/textiles, cartoons, creative writing, dance, drama, games, music, photography, puppetry, and storytelling. Each lesson is organized into three parts:

Goal states the purpose of the activity;

Gather lists the materials required and suggests steps for advance preparation;

Guide contains complete directions for accomplishing the task.

Prayer is for people of all ages—children, youth, and adults. While these designs are intended for young people in classroom settings, they may be easily adapted for use in small and large group worship, education, outreach, and nurture opportunities. They are ideal for parochial school programs, religious education classes, vacation Bible school, Confirmation classes, intergenerational events, youth groups, retreats, family devotions, home schooling, and more.

As you use this resource, may you be as eager and as open as Jesus' disciples were when they pleaded, "Teach us to pray." As you prepare and participate in these activities, may your prayer life be enriched by discovering, or rediscovering, ways to talk with and to listen to God. And as you carry the information and insight from the classroom, home, or parish out to the world, may the power of prayer be reflected in your daily life.

1 God

GOAL

To be used as a "first day" prayer service, and to involve participants in a letter writing project as a way to emphasize the theme "one God."

GATHER

- Bible
- Letter paper (preferably stationery)
- Pens and/or pencils
- Envelopes, 1 per person
- Stickers (decorative, to seal the envelopes)
- Candle and matches
- Tape or CD player, and tape or CD of quiet music

GUIDE

First days mark new beginnings. They offer a time to focus on our relationship with God, and with God's only begotten Son, Jesus. On the first day of a new year, month, liturgical season such as Lent or Advent, or significant event—like the start of school—lead the group in a creative writing activity and prayer ritual based on the theme "one God."

The Old Testament is filled with stories of people who prayed to idols, or gods, of wood or stone. They thought these objects had great power and could hear their prayers. We know that a god of wood or stone has no power, can never answer prayer, and could certainly never love anyone. But God, with a capital "G," can do all these things. Only God can hear us and help us when we pray. Only God loves and sustains us.

Unfortunately, people sometimes have a hard time remembering and believing this simple truth. People create idols, or their own gods, everyday. Modern day idols include things like clothes, hobbies, bikes, cars, superstars, and more. These idols are often worshiped or revered more than the true and only God.

To begin this activity, read aloud Exodus 20:3, "You shall have no other gods before me." Tell the students that this sentence is found in the Bible passage commonly called "the Ten Commandments." Ask the class to identify the number of the Commandment that was just recited. After someone answers "number one," explain that this law is so significant that God put it first on the list.

Next, take time to think about idols and gods that may be part of our lives.

Are things like being on the soccer team, building a great CD collection, or buying the best bike on the top of the list? Are they more important than God? Ask a few of the students to summarize the meaning of the Commandment in simple phrases or sentences, such as "one God."

Invite the students to write a letter, in their own words, highlighting the theme "one God." These letters, addressed to God, are to contain promises to be kept during a designated period of time, such as a season, month, or year. Ideas should center on ways the participants will put God first in their lives.

Give the students an opportunity to formulate thoughts and feelings. Share examples of promises such as "I promise to spend more time reading the Bible than playing video games," or "I promise to give some of my allowance to help someone else." Encourage the young people to be honest and to write about tangible topics such as school, family, and friends, as well as intangible ideas like joy and pain. Distribute paper and pencils and guide the group as they compose their letters.

Once the letters are written, invite the learners to sit in a circle. Light the candle and play quiet background music. Ask the class to share the letters as a group prayer. State that each person, in turn, will have the opportunity to read his or her letter. Since the contents may be very personal, assure the group that they may read their letters out loud or silently. After everyone has had an occasion to share, conclude the ritual with a prayer asking for God's help in keeping the promises.

At the end of the prayer service distribute envelopes, stickers, and pens. Ask the students to address the envelopes to themselves, put the note inside, and seal the letter with a sticker. Collect the projects, and keep them until the end of the designated period of time. You may then give the letters back to the students as a reminder to live a life that honors the one true God.

2 **Prayer Partners**

GOAL

To explore two parts of prayer by painting a mandala, and to form a covenant with another person, as well as with God, to become prayer partners.

GATHER

- Bible
- Bible dictionary or concordance
- Containers for water
- Watercolor paper
- Paint brushes
- Watercolor paint
- Tape or CD player, and tape or CD of nature music

GUIDE

To begin, hold up a Bible and ask the students to name its two main parts: the Old Testament and the New Testament, also referred to as Hebrew Scripture and Christian Scripture. State that in each section of Scripture God provides instruction on prayer. Offer two examples, one from each section of God's Word. Use an Old Testament reference from one of the Psalms, and a New Testament quotation like Matthew 21:22, or look up the word "prayer" in a concordance or Bible dictionary to find additional verses.

Next, ask the group how the number two is connected to the theme of prayer. Explain that prayer is a two-way conversation between a person and God, that involves two parts, talking and listening. To make this theme meaningful for the young people, say that each person will

be given a prayer partner with whom they will make a covenant, or agreement, to give each other spiritual support and care.

Relate examples from Scripture and from real life of this type of bond. Share the Old Testament story of Moses and Aaron's partnership (Exodus 4:14–16), as well as the New Testament account of the relationship between Mary and Elizabeth (Luke 1:39–56). Explain to the young people that partnership can mean different things: there can be a partnership with God or there can be a partnership with another person to God.

If time allows, discuss listening and talking as an important part of any relationship. Ask "When was a time you really listened to what another person had to say? What good came out of listening to

4

another? When was a time when someone really listened to you? How did the two people benefit from the exchange?" Allow students the opportunity to share their experiences with the group.

Organize the group into pairs, and tell each pair that they will become "prayer partners." Explain again that in this type of relationship each person will promise to pray for and with the other individual for a specific period of time, such as a month or a year.

As a way to seal this covenant, invite the partners to paint a mandala together. A mandala is an expression of what an individual feels on the inside while the painting is being created. Explain that both people paint at the same time; however, they do not talk to each other. The painting can be abstract or real, with both individuals contributing to the finished product. Distribute one set of watercolor paints, two brushes, and one piece of watercolor paper to each set of prayer partners.

Once the materials are dispensed, tell the participants to sit quietly with their partners. Play soft, relaxing music and invite the pairs to begin painting whatever comes to their minds. Allow time for work to take place. When all groups have finished, display the artwork for everyone to enjoy.

Conclude the session by suggesting additional opportunities to nurture the prayer partner relationship, together or apart. Partners may agree to pray for each other every morning or evening. They may also arrange to meet at a specific time each week to share joys and concerns.

3 Trinity

GOAL

To propose concrete examples of the concept of the Trinity, and to construct a triptych that will be used as the focal point of a personal worship center.

GATHER

- Examples of "three-in-one" (apple, cube, shamrock, triangle, water)
- Copies of the words to the "Gloria Patri" (see page 8)
- Picture of leader or participant
- Posterboard or construction paper (11" x 14" or 12" x 18")
- Scissors and glue
- Crayons and/or markers
- Pattern for arched panels
- Foil wrapping paper (optional)
- Trims: cording, braid, rickrack (optional)
- Old magazines or greeting cards (optional)

In advance: Prepare the patterns for arched panels, one for each participant.

GUIDE

Apple. Cube. Shamrock. Triangle. Water. Show the students examples of these items and ask the group to name what they have in common. Explain that each object is "three-in-one." It has three parts, and yet it is one thing. Use a cube to illustrate that our world is three-dimensional, containing height and width and depth.

Explain that while we cannot possibly ever know all there is to know about God, Christians believe that God has three ways to help us understand the love, light, and energy God brings to earth. We call this the Trinity, or the three-in-one concept of God: God as

Father, creator of life; God as Jesus, redeemer of life; and God as Spirit, sustainer of life. Explain further that this does not mean we worship three Gods, but that the Trinity is a mystery we accept by faith and understand by experience.

Invite everyone to sing or to look at the words of the "Gloria Patri." This song represents one of the oldest Christian expressions of the understanding of God. Explore the words as an affirmation that God is with us in all ways: as the One who creates and gives us life, as the One who saves us from our faults and sins, and as the One who is ever present with us and gives us power to live in mission to God's world. God has always been and will always be whole and complete, and when we look to God in worship, that wholeness heals our brokenness and makes us one with God and each other.

If possible, hold up a picture of one of the leaders or participants. Explain that a person can be thought of as a father/mother, as a son/daughter, or as a brother/sister, yet he or she is still the same person. It just depends on the relationship being expressed. In the same way, we have different relationships with God. Encourage listeners not to worry if seeing God as three persons, yet as one God, seems confusing. Explain that they are going to participate in an activity to make the message seem more clear.

Tell the participants that they are going to make a triptych, or threefold display, that is an ancient Christian art form. The triptych was used to display three pictures or images about God or Jesus or the disciples, and to remind people of the Trinity. Each picture or image would be displayed in a separate arched panel, yet the three panels were connected.

There are many possible ways to make the idea of the Trinity seem easier to grasp. Relate as many as possible; then allow learners to use those or to develop their own to design their triptychs. Demonstrate or explain each of the following:

Apple
An apple represents the Trinity in that it has three parts: the outer layer or skin, the sweet fruit, and the inner core containing the seeds.

Fleur-de-lis
From French royalty comes this symbol also used as a sign of the Trinity, three flower petals, yet one flower. An iris could be used as the same symbol.

Pottery
A clay pot is an "earthen vessel" like human beings, a trinity created by the potter's skilled hands, the wet clay, and the power of the turning wheel.

Shamrock
Legend says that Saint Patrick explained the Trinity by using the three-leafed shamrock of Ireland, pointing out that it is one plant with one stem, yet has three separate leaves.

Triangle
While it is one distinct shape, a triangle is made of three sides.

Water
Water is two parts hydrogen and one part oxygen, yet that same chemical substance can be experienced in its liquid form or as a solid—ice—or as a vapor—steam.

Allow the participants to choose a symbol or symbols to place on their triptych. They may separate one symbol into its parts and draw them on the different panels, or put a separate symbol on each. Another possibility would be to cut pictures from magazines or use old greeting cards to find symbols to glue on each panel. They may want to write a phrase on each panel suggesting the Trinity, such as the words to the "Gloria Patri," or a prayer such as "In the name of the Father who created us, the Son who redeemed us, and the Holy Spirit who lives in us." Or they may use a different prepositional phrase for each panel: "From the Father, through the Son, by the Holy Spirit."

Demonstrate the process for constructing the triptych. Fold 12" by 18" poster board or construction paper into thirds across the width. Trace an arc pattern to create simple arches at the top of each panel. All three sections can be the same size, or the center panel can be left taller. Adding gold foil paper for a background or trimming with cord, braid, or rickrack will add an elegant touch to the triptych. Add the chosen design to each of the three panels. Once the design is complete, tell the learners to display the triptych as the focal point of a personal worship center for use throughout the entire year.

Note: Throughout the use of this activity, be aware that many churches are making the effort to avoid using only male images to represent God. Use wording or language that reflects the tradition and teaching of the participants. However, the opportunity should be found to explain that God is not male or female, but the creator of both. We use words like "father" because we understand God as our loving parent, the sender of all good gifts. Many cultures represent earth as our "mother," although the Holy Spirit seems to represent many of the "mothering" or nurturing qualities of God.

Gloria Patri
Glory be to the Father, and to the Son, and to the Holy Spirit;
As it was in the beginning, is now and ever shall be,
world without end. Amen.

STEP ONE

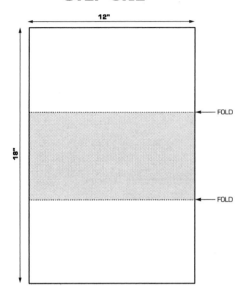

12"

18"

FOLD

FOLD

STEP TWO

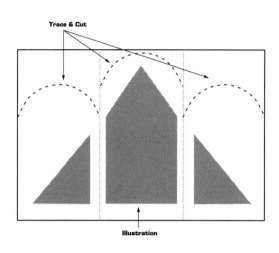

Trace & Cut

Illustration

STEP THREE

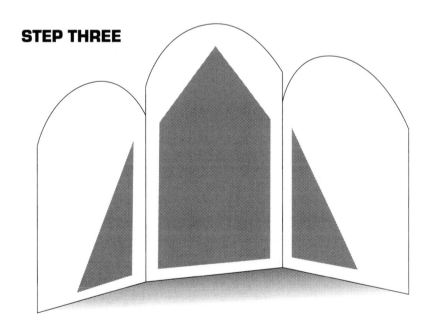

4 Parts of Prayer

GOAL

To explore four basic parts of prayer—adoration, confesssion, thanksgiving, and supplication—and to construct "prayer steps" as a guide for using this formula.

GATHER

- Chalkboard and chalk or newsprint and markers
- Various resource books: prayerbooks, Bibles, dictionaries, and/or hymnals
- Scrap paper
- Pencils or pens
- Construction paper
- Markers

GUIDE

Prayer is the way we talk to God. Sometimes a prayer can be one word, it can be lots of words, or it can just be a feeling in the heart. To help in conversing with God, it is useful to learn that there are four important parts of prayer:

adoration, praising God's greatness;

confession, telling about our actions that did not follow God's law;

thanksgiving, offering thanks for God's love and gifts to us; and

supplication, asking for God's help or guidance.

Although there are many ways to create a prayer, learning a helpful formula showing the basic parts or steps of prayer can be a useful tool for students. Using the first letters of each of the four parts of prayer to form the word ACTS can also serve as a reminder.

Begin by writing "Four _____" on a chalkboard or a sheet of newsprint. As the students arrive have them guess, or print, possible words that are associated with the number "four," for example, the four seasons, the four directions, or the four evangelists. Explain that the answer that fits with this activity is "parts" or "steps." During this lesson the pupils will discover that there are four important parts, or steps, to every prayer.

Organize the students into four groups and assign each cluster one part of prayer: adoration, confession, thanksgiving, and supplication. Supply the teams with resource materials, such as prayerbooks, hymnals, Bibles, and dictionaries. Also provide scrap paper and pencils or pens.

Direct the students to look up their assigned prayer words in the dictionary and to write the definitions on a piece of scrap paper. Instruct the learners to skim through the prayerbooks to find examples of prayers that fit their respective category. Suggest checking hymnals to find songs that have their group's prayer word as a theme. Also recommend that the groups look up specific psalms:

adoration, Psalm 95:1–7;

confession, Psalm 32:1–7;

thanksgiving, Psalm 100;

supplication, Psalm 70:1–3,5.

After a designated period of time, ask each group to share their discoveries about the meaning of their word and specific examples of this type of prayer.

Tell the students that they will be constructing a tool—the ACTS prayer steps—to help them use the four parts of this prayer formula. To begin, have each person choose a favorite color of construction paper. Hold the paper horizon-tally, then fold it into half, then into fourths, then into eighths.

Open up the paper and refold it on the same creases to form steps, or a fan. On the first step, print the word ADORATION, and on the section above it write ways that people demonstrate praise for God. On the next step print CONFESSION, then above it enter something you need to tell God. Print THANKSGIVING on the third step and on the section above, list reasons to be thankful. The last step is SUPPLICATION and the strip above can include anything for which you need God's help.

Suggest that the students fold up their papers and use the craft as a bookmark. They could also stand the steps on a desk or dresser. Remind them that anytime they wish to talk to God, they can use the prayer step idea.

Step 1   Step 2   Step 3

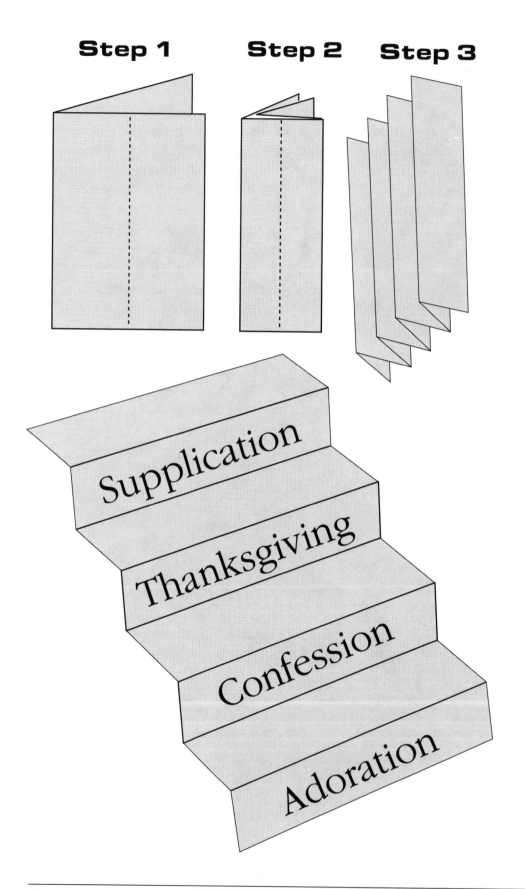

Supplication

Thanksgiving

Confession

Adoration

5 Senses

GOAL

To offer an opportunity to explore sight, sound, smell, taste, and touch through a prayer ritual that incorporates the five senses, and to provide time for journaling on the experience.

GATHER

- Large sheets of newsprint paper
- Markers
- Masking tape
- Pencils
- 8 1/2" x 11" sheets of paper
- Matches

Set up on a table or desktop

- A large bowl filled with water
- Candles (variety of sizes), matches
- Incense
- Tape or CD player, with a tape or CD of Gregorian chant
- A loaf of unleavened bread

In advance: Purchase matzoh wafers at a store, or you can use this recipe to make unleavened bread.

3 cups whole wheat flour	3 tablespoons brown sugar
2/3 cup honey	1 teaspoon salt
1/4 stick butter	9" round pan

Dissolve butter and honey together until they are smooth. Add sugar and salt. Blend evenly with flour, mixing thoroughly. Mixture should be thick. Butter and flour a 9" round pan. Pat the dough into the prepared pan. Bake at 350° for about 30 minutes. After the bread is done, flip it over in the pan, and let it stand in the oven for a few minutes to remove the moisture.

GUIDE

Sight. Sound. Smell. Taste. Touch. God has given us five special gifts through which we experience all of life. Ask the students what these five gifts are usually called. Of course, the answer is the five senses. Invite the young people to offer examples of times when they use their five senses, such as smelling the wonderful cookies Dad is baking, tasting a gooey brownie, or petting a fluffy dog.

Organize the learners into five groups. Assign one of the senses to each team, and give them each a piece of newsprint and a marker. Explain that each group is to list on the newsprint gifts of God that are experienced with the sense they have been assigned—sight, sound, smell, taste, or touch.

Remind the participants that this is a time of brainstorming. The goal is to compile a long list, not to be concerned about right and wrong answers. Give a five minute or less time frame, and a "ready, set, go" signal to begin. When the minutes are up, use the masking tape to display each group's list for the others to see. Allow an opportunity to share responses.

Next, help the learners think about how their senses are used in church. Replies may include seeing candles, hearing music, or smelling flowers. Instruct the five groups to brainstorm and record as many ideas as possible on another piece of newsprint. At the conclusion of the designated period, allow time for sharing answers.

Regather as one group. Prepare a table as the focal point for a prayer ritual by placing the following items on it: a large bowl of water, a loaf of unleavened bread, a variety of candles, an incense stick, and a tape player containing a recording of Gregorian chant music. Arrange the objects in a prayerful, creative way.

Give the young people an opportunity to experience each item through the gift of sight, smell, sound, taste, and touch. Ignite the candle and pause to reflect on the sight. Light the incense and take time to smell the fragrance. Play the tape and allow the opportunity to enjoy its timeless sound and its echoing voices. While the music plays, invite the partici-

pants to come up, one at a time, to dip their hands into the water, then make the sign of the cross on their foreheads. When everyone is seated, break and share the bread with each person.

After a time of silent reflection, distribute several sheets of 8 1/2" x 11" paper to each participant, along with pencils. Instruct the learners to form a journal by folding the papers in half. Direct the group to record what they experienced through their five senses during the prayer ritual. Ask questions such as these: What did you think of when you saw the candles burning? How did the bread taste to you? Did it remind you of anything? Did you like the smell of the incense? Have you ever heard Gregorian chant before? Did you like the way it sounded? What did it sound like? Was the water cold or warm to the touch? How does water feel? Does water feel different at different times?

Provide time for the learners to record their thoughts and feelings in their journals. Continue the activity by inviting the students to complete the following sentence starters:

Prayer looks like…
Prayer sounds like…
Prayer smells like…
Prayer tastes like…
Prayer feels like….

Invite anyone who feels comfortable to share his or her responses with the entire group.

6 Jars of Water

GOAL

To recall the story of Jesus' first miracle—turning water into wine—and to use the theme of water in six prayer activities.

GATHER

- Bible
- Paper and pens
- Materials related to six various activities listed below
- *For optional activity:* Self-hardening clay, toothpicks, and 6 strips of paper

GUIDE

Count the letters in the word "prayer." There are six of them. Six is also a number associated with a special event that took place in Jesus' early ministry. This incident, recorded in John 2:1–11, is commonly referred to as the "miracle at Cana." Share the Gospel account of this story with your class, or read them the version that follows:

When Jesus, Mary, and the disciples were guests at a wedding in the town of Cana of Galilee, the host of the celebration ran out of wine. Mary immediately prompted Jesus to do something about the situation. Jesus noticed that there were stone jars—six of them—generally used for the Jewish rite of purification. Jesus told the servants to fill the jars with water. Then he told them to draw some of the liquid out of the containers. When the servants tasted the substance they discovered that Jesus had turned the water to wine!

Jesus used water to perform his first miracle. Actually, water *is* a miracle! Water is the substance that sustains life for everything in God's creation.

After sharing the story of the wedding at Cana with the students, engage them in a prayer activity focusing on the theme of water. There are actually six parts to this activity. These can be done within one class, or you can divide up the six for use during several classes or times. (On page 17, you'll find directions for an optional activity to begin these experiences.)

One: Recall Scripture Stories

Direct the group to locate six Scripture stories related to the theme of water. Suggestions include:

Genesis 1–2:3 *the story of creation;*
Genesis 5:1–9:17 *Noah and the ark;*
Exodus 14:1–21 *Moses at the Red Sea;*
Jonah 1–2 *Jonah and the whale;*

Matthew 3:13–17 *Jesus' baptism*;
John 2:1–11 *Jesus at Cana*.
Offer a prayer of thanks for ways in which water has been used to teach us more about God, Jesus, and the Holy Spirit.

Two: Uses for Water

Invite the group to name six uses of water. Suggest categories rather than specifics, such as:

> *farming*
> *drinking*
> *recreation*
> *medicinal*
> *cleaning*
> *industrial.*

Lead the group in spontaneous prayer thanking God for ways that water is part of our lives.

Three: Songs about Water

Sing a few songs related to the theme of water. Some suggestions are:

"I've Got Peace Like a River"
"Peace Is Flowing Like a River"
"Wide, Wide as the Ocean"
"Raindrops Keep Falling on my Head"
"Rain, Rain, Go Away"
"Bridge over Troubled Water"

Conclude by singing "Praise God from Whom All Blessings Flow," concentrating on the theme of water as a gift from God.

Four: Conservation Methods

Explain to the class the need for water conservation. Challenge the group to name six ways to preserve this important resource. Possible answers are:

—take short showers
—plant trees
—use water saving appliances
—wash only full loads of clothes
—repair leaks
—sweep rather than hose sidewalks.

Guide the group in praying that they may be good stewards of God's gift, water.

Five: Sharing Memories of Water

Share memories of experiences in which water was the focus. Ask each person to relate a remembrance based on these six, or other, suggestions:

> *fun*
> *people*
> *pets*
> *thirst*
> *vacation*
> *places.*

Use a prayer where each person interjects one word at a time, recounting memories of water-related experiences.

Six: Discover More about Water

Share information about service projects that offer water to "thirsty" people:

—homeless centers
—soup kitchens
—world relief organizations
—irrigation projects
—fish farms
—agricultural education.

Pray for people who share God's love by participating in water related projects.

At the conclusion of the six activities, suggest that the students use the information and ideas to remember the importance of God's wondrous gift of water.

Optional Activity

Since there were six jars involved with Jesus' first miracle, you can have your class create six simple clay containers for use during this activity. (Or, you can make the jars yourself, ahead of time.)

To start, provide six balls of self-hardening clay, and give one ball to each of six students. Have them place the ball of clay in the palm of the hand, and gently rotate the material around until it becomes pliable and easy to shape. Form a small jar from the clay and press an opening into the center of it. (Note that the jars do not have to be identical in size or shape.)

When the six jars are completed, use a toothpick to scratch a number from one to six on the outside of each jar. Allow time for the jars to harden.

While the six students are making the jars, you can give six small strips of paper to another six students. Instruct them to write one of the following phrases on each piece, along with a number from one to six:

1. Recall Scripture stories
2. Suggest uses
3. Sing songs
4. Name conservation methods
5. Share memories
6. Discover information.

These strips of paper will then be rolled up, and each placed into the jar with the corresponding number, when the jars have hardened.

Then, depending on when you want to do your activities (e.g., in one class, several classes, or one a month), have the students remove the paper from each jar, beginning with one and ending with six, and participate in the related project.

7 Gifts of the Spirit

GOAL

To use guided meditation as a way to help participants discern the seven gifts of the Spirit—wisdom, understanding, knowledge, fortitude (courage), counsel (right judgment), piety (reverence), and fear of the Lord (wonder and awe).

GATHER

- Newsprint and markers
- Bible
- Seven candles in a variety of sizes and colors; matches
- Reference books with information about the "gifts of the Spirit" (optional)

GUIDE

The Holy Spirit, third person of the Trinity, bestows upon Christians seven special characteristics. These are traditionally referred to as the "gifts of the Spirit": wisdom, understanding, knowledge, fortitude (courage), counsel (right judgment), piety (reverence), and fear of the Lord (wonder and awe). Listed in various places in the New Testament, especially 1Corinthians 12:8–10, and prophesied in the Old Testament in Isaiah 11:1–3, God has shared these gifts with us by sending the Spirit to help us live Christlike lives.

Using newsprint and markers, challenge the students to identify the seven historical gifts of the Spirit. Write the names of the "gifts" they identify, even if incorrect. Ask the learners to explain why they chose the gifts they mentioned. Once all the pupils have had an opportunity to participate, write the seven gifts on a clean sheet of newsprint.

Then, read the Scripture passages given below, and use them as a guide for discussion about each of the gifts.

Wisdom

The Lord gives wisdom. Proverbs 2:6

Wisdom helps us make right decisions and guides us from doing wrong. Wisdom is a gift people build up through experience. A wise person knows what to do in many situations. A wise believer sees the people and events of human history fitting together in the large plan of God's love.

Understanding

Give me understanding so I may keep your law with all my heart. Psalm 119:34

Understanding helps us discover what the stories in the Bible, especially Jesus' instructions, have to teach us. Understanding is the gift of thinking and reflecting on experience. People with understanding think things through for themselves and act on their insights.

Knowledge

The earth shall be filled with the knowledge of the Lord. Isaiah 11:9

The gift of knowledge helps us to know Jesus as our friend and to comprehend what is needed to serve God. Knowledge is a gift for seeking out the facts and information necessary to make wise and fair decisions.

Fortitude (Courage)

Be strong in the Lord and in the strength of his power. Ephesians 6:10

This gift helps us to love God and others and to do what God wants us to do, even when we are afraid. Courage is the strength to do what isn't always easy, to stand up for the unpopular, to speak the truth, to put one's self on the line for what is right.

Counsel (Right Judgment)

How wonderful is the Lord's judgment. Isaiah 28:29

This gift helps us to lead others in knowing what is right and wrong, and how to be courageous in doing what is right. Counsel is a willingness to consider the insights and understandings of others about a situation and to work together towards a solution.

(Piety) Reverence

Reverence the Lord Christ in your heart. 1 Peter 3:15

Reverence helps us to show our love for God, for God's people, and God's earth in our words and actions. Reverence is the gift of honoring God and others. The pious person reveres and worships God. The pious person has reverence for all people with the respect we want for ourselves.

Fear of the Lord (Wonder/Awe)

Reverence the holy One and be in awe of the God of Israel. Isaiah 29:23

This gift helps us put God first in everything we say and do and show respect for God's holy name and all of creation. Fear of the Lord is the gift of awe and wonder at God's life-giving and life-sustaining presence in creation and in us.

Discuss ways in which these statements reflect the journey of life. Share the following lines:

- I am seeking wisdom.
- I see a need for a deep understanding.
- I know I need good judgment to be the best I can be.
- I could use a good dose of courage, too.
- Knowledge won't come easily. I have to work for it.
- I really want to be respectful and reverent.
- It can be wonderful and awesome to be alive and to have faith.

Tell the group that they will participate in a guided meditation as a way of reflecting on each of the seven gifts of the Spirit. Invite the participants to form a circle on the floor or on chairs, and to sit in a comfortable position. Place the seven candles in the center of the circle. Name each of the seven gifts, lighting one candle after naming each of the gifts.

Before beginning the meditation, invite the students to pray the following words, repeating each line:

Come, Holy Spirit,
Fill the hearts of your people
And enkindle in them
the fire of your love.
Send forth your Spirit
And you shall renew the face of the earth.

GUIDED MEDITATION

Continue the prayer experience by reading the guided meditation below, slowly and prayerfully.

God the Holy Spirit, the third person of the Trinity, is with us today. To help us, the Holy Spirit gives us special gifts so that this day and every day we can make good decisions.

The Holy Spirit gives us wisdom (light the first candle). Think for a moment of a time when you knew what God wanted of you and you did it. See in your mind what it was that you did.

The Holy Spirit gives us understanding (light the second candle). Think of a time when you showed compassion and understanding toward another person. What was the situation? Recall it in your mind.

The Holy Spirit gives us the gift of counsel or right judgment (light the third candle). Think of a time when you made the right decision. In your mind, see who was involved in this decision. Was it many people, or just you and God?

The Holy Spirit gives us courage, also called fortitude (light the fourth candle). Think of a time when you did something that took a lot of courage. Perhaps it was standing up for something you believed in. In your mind and heart, what did it feel like? Were you afraid?

The Spirit gives us the gift of knowledge (light the fifth candle). Think of a time when you had clear knowledge of God and your faith. See once again how God was made known.

The Spirit gives us piety (light the sixth candle). Think of a time when you were filled with a deep love for God. In your mind, see where God is in your life. Do you feel God's presence right now?

The Holy Spirit gives us the gift of wonder and awe (light the seventh candle). Think of a time when you were filled with wonder and awe at God's creation. In your mind, see your favorite place in the world. With your eyes closed be in that place for a moment or two. Give thanks for God's wonderful gifts.

Now, let us think about what we have just heard and visualized. Open your eyes when you are ready.

(Conclude the session by reciting the following prayer from the Rite of Confession #25:)

All powerful God, the Father of our Lord Jesus Christ, by water and the Holy Spirit you freed your sons and daughters from sin and gave them new life. Send your Holy Spirit upon them to be their helper and guide. Give them the spirit of wisdom and understanding, the spirit of right judgment and courage, the spirit of knowledge and reverence. Fill them with the spirit of wonder and awe in your presence. We ask this through Christ, our Lord. Amen.

8 Beatitudes

GOAL

To participate in different prayer postures, and to experience a deeper understanding of the eight Beatitudes.

GATHER

- A copy of the Beatitudes (Matthew 5:3–10) for each person
- White paper; one sheet per person
- Pencils or pens
- Tape or CD, with player, of quiet background music

GUIDE

An overture introduces and plays various themes of the symphony or music that follows. A hint here…full promise there…a startling burst of color. So it is with the Beatitudes. They are the overture to the Sermon on the Mount.

Begin by asking the students questions about the Sermon on the Mount. Why was the Sermon so important? What was Jesus saying in this message? What are the Beatitudes? Name the eight Beatitudes. How do the Beatitudes ask us to be different? Why do you think Jesus gave us the Beatitudes? Encourage discussion before distributing copies of the Beatitudes to the participants.

Pass out a copy of the Beatitudes to each learner. Invite eight participants to read the Beatitudes aloud. Encourage dialogue after each Beatitude is read. Guide the group in thinking about what Jesus' words mean for people today. Use the following to direct the conversation.

Blessed are the poor in spirit, for theirs is the kingdom of heaven.

To be poor in spirit is to remember that we cannot depend on things or possessions, but only on God and God's unfailing love.

Blessed are they who mourn, for they will be comforted.

To mourn is to be sad and to sometimes cry when we see people who are hurting and in pain because of sin, hatred, sickness, death, poverty, war, or injustice.

Blessed are the meek, for they shall inherit the land.

To be meek is to be humble and to realize that all our gifts, talents, and abilities come from God. We need to use them to do good for others and to make a better world for all people.

Blessed are they who hunger and thirst for righteousness, for they will be satisfied.

To hunger and thirst for righteousness is to have a great desire to do what God requires of us—to see that justice is carried out. It is to work for good relationships between people and peace in the whole world.

Blessed are the merciful, for they will be shown mercy.

To be merciful is to show love and compassion to people in need and to forgive those who hurt us.

Blessed are the clean of heart, for they shall see God.

To be clean of heart is to put God first in our lives and to do what we know is right.

Blessed are the peacemakers, for they will be called children of God.

To be a peacemaker is to always try to be reconciled or at peace with others, even if they are our enemies. To forgive and to be forgiven is very important in being a peacemaker.

Blessed are they who are persecuted for the sake of righteousness, for theirs is the kingdom of heaven.

To be persecuted because we do what God asks is to have the strength and courage to do what Jesus teaches us, no matter who ridicules or punishes us for living as Jesus lived.

As a way to further illustrate the Beatitudes and to provide a prayer experience based on Jesus' important words, invite the students to be seated on the floor. Dim the lights and put on soft music. Encourage and lead the participants in a different prayer posture, or gesture, for each of the Beatitudes.

Blessed are the poor in spirit, for theirs is the kingdom of heaven. Fold arms across chest. Extend arms toward heaven.

Blessed are they who mourn, for they will be comforted. Places hands over face. Embrace shoulders.

Blessed are the meek, for they shall inherit the land. Kneel, arms down, palms out, toward earth.

Blessed are they who hunger and thirst for righteousness, for they will be satisfied. Stretch out arms and hands. Stand.

Blessed are the merciful, for they will be shown mercy. Bow head with hands folded in prayer.

Blessed are the clean of heart, for they shall see God. Cup hands over the heart, head up with eyes open to heaven.

Blessed are the peacemakers, for they will be called children of God. Make a circle by joining hands. Lift hands over head.

Blessed are they who are persecuted for the sake of righteousness, for theirs is the kingdom of heaven. Kneel with hands outstretched in front of body. Stand with head and hands toward heaven.

Once the exercise is completed, invite the students to sit quietly and to reflect on the experience. After an appropriate time, distribute a piece of paper and a pencil to each person. Tell the pupils to record their thoughts and feelings about what they learned from the Beatitudes and from praying Jesus' teachings through gesture and movement. If individuals feel comfortable sharing their responses, encourage conversation from the group at the conclusion of the activity.

9 Fruits of the Spirit

GOAL

To review the nine fruits of the spirit—love, joy, peace, patience, kindness, goodness, faithfulness, gentleness, and self-control—and to dramatize stories of biblical, historical, and contemporary people who evidence these in their lives.

GATHER

- Bibles and other resource materials on persons of faith
- Paper and pencils/pens
- Nine candles of varying colors and sizes; matches
- Costumes and props for skits (optional)

GUIDE

Galatians 5:22–23 identifies nine fruits of the Spirit. Look up the passage and read the list to the class: love, joy, peace, patience, kindness, goodness, faithfulness, gentleness, and self-control. Explain that the fruits of the Spirit are the outward expressions of faith in a person's life; they are the external evidence of the work of the Holy Spirit in the life of a believer. The fruits of the Spirit are also characteristics displayed by people of prayer.

Challenge the students to think of people whose lives exhibit love, joy, peace, patience, kindness, goodness, faithfulness, gentleness, and self-control. Tell the students that they will use Scripture stories, biographical information, and resource materials to match a biblical, historical, or contemporary person of prayer with each fruit of the Spirit. Provide examples to start the project, such as:

Love
Biblical: Jesus
Historical: Saint Margaret of Scotland
Contemporary: Mother Teresa

Joy
Biblical: Elizabeth, cousin of Mary
Historical: Saint Nicholas
Contemporary: Amy Grant

Peace
Biblical: Noah
Historical: Saint Francis
Contemporary: Gandhi

Patience
Biblical: Job
Historical: Annie Sullivan (Helen Keller's teacher)
Contemporary: Corrie Ten Boom

Kindness
Biblical: Abraham
Historical: Clara Barton
Contemporary: Jane Addams

Goodness

Biblical: Lydia

Historical: Abraham Lincoln

Contemporary: Jimmy Carter

Faithfulness

Biblical: Ruth

Historical: Saint Patrick

Contemporary: Oscar Romero

Gentleness

Biblical: Mary

Historical: Anne Frank

Contemporary: Eleanor Roosevelt

Self-control

Biblical: Paul

Historical: Dietrich Bonhoeffer

Contemporary: Martin Luther King, Jr.

Have the students work on this project in one of the following ways: Participants may work individually, finding one example for each characteristic; or, the students may work in small groups with each team identifying a person for each "fruit"; or, each group can name a person for one specific "fruit." Another option is to have one group research biblical people, another group identify historical individuals, and the third group study contemporary men, women, and children.

Provide Bibles and resource books, as well as paper and pencils or pens, to all students or groups. Guide the students as they search the Scriptures and other resources to gather information on the people they select.

Once the information has been compiled, regather the large group. Make a list of the people that were identified for each fruit of the Spirit. Take time to talk about ways in which the characteristic is evi-denced in the person's life; for example, Mother Teresa demonstrates love through her self-sacrificing work with the poor. Ruth displays faithfulness by remaining with her mother-in-law, Naomi.

Choose one person on the list to illustrate each quality—love, joy, peace, patience, kindness, goodness, faithfulness, gentleness, and self-control—by asking the participants to vote by raising their hands, applauding, or voicing their opinions. Try to include three biblical, three historical, and three contemporary examples in the final selections.

Option: *You can do this section ahead of time by finding information yourself on one person of faith for each fruit of the Spirit. Write a short biography for each person that the students can then use to plan a brief skit to present during classtime. If you'd like, you can collect a few costume and prop suggestions for each skit.*

When the information has been gathered, organize the class into nine groups and assign one fruit of the Spirit/person of prayer to each team. Explain to the teams that they are to develop a brief sketch of the life of the person their group has been given. Here are some dramatic methods that can be used:

characterization of Bible passage
first person account
improvisation
interview
masks
mime
news report
role playing
a tableau.

Some of these methods may require more advance preparation than others, so plan according to the time and need of your particular situation.

Provide time and materials, and help the small groups prepare their presentations for the prayer service. When the participants are ready, assemble the students in an area prepared for the worship experience.

To start, tell the group that they will participate in a prayer service thanking God for the examples of people who demonstrate the fruits of the Spirit in their lives. Tell the group that each fruit of the Spirit will be named and a candle lit at the same time. At that point, the people who prepared the drama illustrating that characteristic will come forward, offer their brief performance, and return to their seats. After the drama, a time of silent reflection on the life and lesson of the person will be observed.

Begin the service by lighting the first candle and saying "The first fruit of the Spirit is love." Invite the participants who prepared the "love" segment to present their dramatic sketch. After the story, allow time for silent reflection on the message. Invite the group to respond with the words: "Thank you, God for the example of [name person]. Help us to show love in our lives."

Repeat the process until the nine candles have been lit, the nine gifts have been named, and the nine dramas have been presented. Conclude by rereading Galatians 5:22–23 for the group.

10 Commandments

GOAL

To use an action story as a way to review the Ten Commandments and respond to God's laws as guidelines for prayer.

GATHER

- Ten Commandments action story
- Newsprint or chalkboard (optional)
- Marker(s) or chalk (optional)

GUIDE

Prayer is one method of expressing love for God and for others. Living a life based on the Ten Commandments is another. In Exodus 20:1–17 and Deuteronomy 5:1–21, God gives us instructions which help us show love for our Creator and for all human beings.

Jesus summarized the Old Testament laws with the New Testament words "Love God with all your heart, and your neighbor as yourself" (Matthew 22:37–40). Communicating love for God and for others, through adoration, confession, thanksgiving, and supplication, should be the essence of every prayer.

In this lesson, you will study the Ten Commandments and help the students make a commitment to live according to God's guidelines. Although it is useful to memorize key passages from Scripture, it is more important to understand the meaning behind the words. This action story helps students comprehend the Ten Commandments in a unique and positive way. It involves the learner in the process, and assures that the Bible story is memorable and meaningful.

After explaining the theme of the lesson, have the group sit or stand facing the leader, who tells the story and demonstrates the motions for the participants. You can make copies of the Commandment verses ahead of time to distribute to class members, or write the words on a piece of newsprint or on a chalkboard. Or, students can simply repeat the lines of the verses after the leader. Additional movements and gestures may be improvised by the group or the leader, as desired.

Raise one finger...
Commandment number one
Is simple to recall:
There is only one God
Jehovah, Lord of all.

Raise two fingers...
God's name is very special
Hold it in high regard.

That's commandment number two.
It isn't very hard.

Raise three fingers…
Sunday is a special day
Do not work, but rest.
The third commandment tells us
That Sunday is the best.

Raise four fingers…
Your father and your mother
Are gifts from God to you.
Commandment number four says
Honor them in all you do.

Raise five fingers…
Do not murder, God tells us
In commandment number five.
The special creatures God has made
Must all be kept alive.

Raise six fingers…
Be faithful to the one you love
Is six's guide for life.
This is a good commandment
For a husband and a wife.

Raise seven fingers…
Commandment seven says do not take
What does not belong to you.
By keeping this commandment
You praise God in all you do.

Raise eight fingers…
Bear no false witness, number eight,
Means in everything you do
Tell the truth about others
It is God's law for you.

Raise nine fingers…
Do not desire your neighbor's wife;
That's commandment number nine.
If we're satisfied with what we have
God's love, through us, can shine.

Raise ten fingers…
There may be things that others have
That you'd like to have, too.
Number ten says do not covet;
This is God's guide for you.

At the conclusion of the action story ask the group to name ways that the Ten Commandments are connected with the topic of prayer. Of course, everyone needs to pray for God's help and guidance in keeping the laws. And, since we cannot keep the Commandments perfectly, we must pray for forgiveness when we break them. Most importantly, be sure the students understand that the theme of love for God and for others, as outlined in the Ten Commandments, must be the basis for all prayer.

11 The Lord's Prayer

GOAL

Through the use of creative writing and mantra, to take a closer look at the Lord's Prayer, the model for all Christian prayer.

GATHER

- Newsprint and markers
- Masking tape
- Bibles (one per student, optional)

GUIDE

Often, the Lord's Prayer is repeated routinely, by rote. When this happens, it becomes nothing more than empty words, and unfortunately, Jesus' important teachings are missed. The Lord's Prayer—Jesus' lesson to us on prayer—is an affirmation of God's abundant and unending love for his children. This learning activity will help participants meditate on each petition, and will encourage a better understanding of the words of this wonderful guide for our devotional life.

Ask the students to identify the only prayer in the Bible that Jesus taught us to pray. Wait for answers. Once the Lord's Prayer has been mentioned, ask if anyone knows where it is located in the New Testament. To help the pupils, distribute Bibles at this time. If the learners are having difficulty finding the verses, suggest that they look in Luke's Gospel. Ask them to continue the search. If the

participants still need help, direct them to chapter 11. The Lord's Prayer is at the beginning of this chapter. Ask participants to read Luke 11:2-4 silently. Once all have read the passage, invite one student to read the verses out loud to the entire group.

With the use of newsprint and markers, print one line of the Lord's Prayer on the top of eleven pieces of paper. The lines should be written as follows:

- *Our Father, you are in heaven...*
- *Holy is your name...*
- *Your kingdom come...*
- *Your will be done...*
- *On earth...*
- *As it is in heaven...*
- *Give us this day our daily bread...*
- *And forgive us our trespasses...*
- *As we forgive those who trespass against us...*
- *And lead us not into temptation...*
- *But deliver us from evil.*

Tape the newsprint sheets, in order, around the walls of the room.

Invite the students to continue exploring the meaning of the Lord's Prayer by adding their own words after each of the eleven lines. This may be done as an individual or group project, depending on the size of the class. For example, the entire group may discuss ideas and one person may write responses on the sheets, or small groups of two or three students may be assigned to record their thoughts on one specific piece of newsprint.

For an individual project, ask each pupil to stand at a different piece of paper. At a designated signal, instruct the participants to write their thoughts on the assigned theme. Time the activity, and after one minute, direct the students to move one sheet to the right and to repeat the process. Continue the activity until each person has had the opportunity to record responses for each of the eleven phrases.

Here are some examples of the types of responses the students may give:

- *Our Father, you are in heaven...*
  You are our only God.
  Jesus asked us to call you "Father," and so we do.
  You look after our world.
  You are the one who, out of love, gave us our life.
  You wait for the day to see all your people in heaven.

- *Holy is your name...*
  All of creation is holy and good because of your awesome power and goodness.

Blessed and holy is your name, you who are the source of all love.
Help us remember we can do nothing without you.
Abba, Father, we love your name.

- *Your kingdom come...*
  We try hard at building your kingdom.
  Your kingdom, a place where all people will live in harmony with one another and with your wonderful earth.
  Your kingdom, a place where peace and understanding will be the rule.

- *Your will be done...*
  Your will, not mine, Lord.
  If you lead I will go, I will follow in your way.
  Father, you gave us a free will.
    Help us to do our part in changing this imperfect world.
  Make my heart as yours, open and willing, one and the same.
  Your will be done in my life.

- *On earth...*
  On earth, yes, Lord, may all that you stood for be lived out here on earth.
  We want our life on earth to please you.
  We know, dear God, and we have experienced pieces of your kingdom here on earth.

- *As it is in heaven...*
  Heaven, God? Sometimes I wonder. There's so much pain, so much hate, so much violence in this world.
  We know you're there, somewhere. In heaven?

- *Give us this day our daily bread...*
  Each day is a gift.
  Give us the hope we need to understand.

Continue to feed us with the goodness of your life, the life of Jesus, who came to give food to all people.

Bread for weary travelers; soul food.

Give to us today and all our days the compassion to feed those who have no hope.

• *And forgive us our trespasses...*

God, we have done wrong, we have hurt others, we have not loved.

Help those we have hurt to forgive us.

Help us to forgive ourselves.

We fail most of the time at not seeing Jesus in other people.

We have lied and shown hate.

Fill us with virtue, help us to love in all ways.

Look into our hearts and find the goodness.

We ask to be forgiven.

• *As we forgive those who trespass against us...*

To do as Jesus did is difficult at times.

To forgive isn't easy.

What! When someone hurts me and puts me down, I need to forgive?!

Help us in this forgiveness thing.

Help us to see and accept the weakness in others.

Help us to realize that imperfection is a part of being human.

In a world where ME and I are most important, and US and WE are a thing of the past, help us to put things into the proper perspective.

• *And lead us not into temptation...*

We need your help, Lord.

Temptation is all around us.

We pray that we will be spared the allures of evil.

We recall how Jesus was tempted, but never gave in.

Lead us into that same strength.

Lead us onto the right path: the path of courage and compassion.

• *But deliver us from evil. Amen.*

Evil seems to be all around us.

This is not the world you want.

Drugs, killing, hate, using other people for our own pleasure, lying, stealing—all these things come so easy.

Lord, the evil one is all around, waiting to take us in.

Deliver us from all that is evil, and bring all of life to holy completion.

Once the creative writing activity is completed, take time to review the ideas recorded on each sheet of newsprint. As a conclusion to this unique learning experience, invite the participants to sit in a circle and lead the group in a mantra, or chant, of the Lord's Prayer. Slowly and thoughtfully say each line of the prayer, asking the students to meditatively and reflectively repeat each line as it is spoken. End the activity with a quiet dismissal.

12 The Apostles' Creed

GOAL

To explore the twelve articles of the Apostles' Creed through participation in an architecture/art project, and to incorporate rubbings into a year-long prayer calendar.

GATHER

- Paper, 11" x 17" newsprint or large white paper, 7 sheets per person
- White paper, 5 1/2" x 8 1/2"
- Markers and crayons
- Stapler and staples
- Scissors, glue, and masking tape

In advance...

- Write each article of the Apostles' Creed on a separate sheet of newsprint. (You can divide the phrases of the Apostles' Creed as shown in the Guide section below.)
- Collect objects relevant to the articles of the Apostles' Creed.
- Select details in a church or school that will make interesting rubbings: plaques, cornerstones, engravings, and the like.
- Request permission to use objects in the church or school for this activity.

GUIDE

Since the Bible is so important to our faith, many people try to memorize parts of Scripture. To help in this practice, early Christians wrote statements based on the truths in God's Word that people could memorize. These statements were called "creeds," short declarations of belief. One often-used creed is the Apostles' Creed, twelve articles that sum-marize the most important scriptural teachings of the Apostles, Jesus' first disciples.

Challenge the students to recite the Apostles' Creed in a unique way. Divide the students into twelve teams (if the class is small, the students can do this individually). Give each team or person one piece of newsprint with an article of the Apostles' Creed written on it. Direct the participants to line up in the order the phrases appear in the creed. In other words, the student or group with the words "I believe in God, the Father almighty…" should be at the beginning of the line, and the pupil or team with the phrase "And the life everlasting…" should be at the end of the queue.

Give a "ready, set, go" signal, and guide the players as they complete the sequencing activity. Once the pupils and the phrases are arranged, ask each group to read the words they are holding.

Suggest that one way to remember the words of each article of the Apostles' Creed is to associate a symbol with it. Instruct each group to reread the words they are holding and direct the students to try to think of a symbol that could represent the phrase. Encourage the learners to help each other with suggestions. Possible symbols include:

• *I believe in God, the Father almighty, creator of heaven and earth…*
an Alpha and an Omega, a world

• *I believe in Jesus Christ, his only Son, our Lord…*
IHS, the first letters of Jesus' name in Greek capitals, XP, the first two letters of the Greek word for Christ

• *Who was conceived by the Holy Spirit, born of the Virgin Mary…*
lily, manger

• *Suffered under Pontius Pilate, was crucified, died, and was buried. He descended to the dead…*
crown of thorns, lamb

• *On the third day he rose again…*
butterfly, open tomb

• *He ascended into heaven, and he is seated at the right hand of God, the Father…*
cloud, crown

• *And he will come to judge the living and the dead…*
fire, trumpet

• *I believe in the Holy Spirit…*
dove, triangle

• *The holy, catholic church, the communion of saints…*
fish, ship

• *The forgiveness of sins…*
chalice, cross

• *The resurrection of the body…*
phoenix, wheat

• *And the life everlasting…*
circle, olive tree

One way to represent the symbols for the Apostles' Creed is to make a rubbing. A rubbing is an ancient art form that captures architectural details on paper. Explain that each person will rub a symbol for each phrase of the Creed. Later, the artwork will be combined into a twelve-month calendar activity as a way to help illustrate the twelve articles.

Demonstrate the process for making a rubbing. Place thin paper over the symbol and use masking tape to hold the paper in place (be careful not to put the tape on any surface the adhesive may pull up, like paint). Rub firmly over the paper using a crayon held on its side. Use broad strokes until the complete image appears.

Gather the group in the location where the rubbings will be done. If possible, use the inside and the outside of the church or school so the architectural details of the building can be incorporated into the rubbings. This project may also be executed around tables or on the floor by providing objects to trace. Supply paper and crayons and guide the students as they work.

Once the pupils have completed twelve rubbings, regather the group and provide instructions for combining the art projects into a twelve-month calendar—one page for each article of the Creed. Furnish seven pieces of paper for each calendar. Large size paper such as 11" x 17" allows the students room for the illustrations.

Fold the seven pages in half and staple the sheets in the middle, on the crease line. Use the twelve top sections of the calendar to mount the symbols. Note that

the emblems may have to be trimmed to fit in the space. Tell the participants to write the words of the respective article of the Creed on the sheet.

To make the pages for each month, dates may be copied off another calendar, or calendar pages may be duplicated and glued to the bottom of each respective sheet. Design a cover which includes the words "The Apostles' Creed."

Tell the students to display their completed calendars in a place that will remind them the Apostles' Creed is our statement of what we believe about God's Word and God's promises. The Apostles' Creed, and the symbols associated with each article, help us to say easily and quickly what we believe as Christians.

13 Disciples

GOAL

To review information about Jesus' thirteen disciples—the original twelve, plus Matthias—and to create newspapers containing examples of their experiences of prayer.

GATHER

- Bibles (at least 5)
- Newsprint, 12" x 18" construction paper, or 11" x 17" white paper
- Pencils, pens, markers, and crayons
- Paper (white and construction)
- Scissors
- Glue

GUIDE

"Extra! Extra! Read all about it! Special edition on Jesus' disciples!" Invite the participants to become reporters and to create newspapers containing information about Jesus and his special followers. Begin by asking how many disciples Jesus had. Most likely, participants will answer "twelve." Twelve is a correct answer, since at any one time there were twelve disciples.

Actually, though, thirteen men were chosen to be the special helpers of Jesus. Ask the pupils to try to name them: Simon Peter, Andrew, James, John, Philip, Bartholomew, Matthew, Thomas, James the Less, Jude Thaddaeus, Simon the Zealot, Judas Iscariot, and Matthias, Judas's replacement.

Remind the students that a disciple is a pupil or follower of a teacher or school. The thirteen disciples referred to in this activity were the early followers of Jesus, and were often called the Apostles. One of Jesus' most notable teachings to this group was on the topic of prayer. Prayer was an important part of Jesus' life. In fact, because the selection of the first disciples was such a significant consideration, Jesus spent the entire night praying to God the Father before coming to a decision. Read the passage about this incident (Luke 6:12–13) to the class.

Organize the reporters into five groups to learn more about the theme of prayer. Provide each team with a Bible, paper, and pencils or pens, and assign one of the Gospels and Acts to each group. Tell the students that these books record what Jesus teaches us about prayer—why we should pray, how to pray, and when to pray.

Direct the participants to scan their assigned book to find examples of prayer involving Jesus and the disciples. Choices can include: Matthew 6:9–15, Jesus teaches the disciples to pray; Mark 14:22–26, Jesus prays at the Last Supper; Luke 22:39–46, Jesus prays in Gethsemane; John 17:20–26, Jesus prays for all his followers; Acts 1:12–26, the disciples pray before choosing a replacement.

Using a newspaper format, instruct each group to create and complete projects for their own edition of *The Galilee Gazette*. Provide each team with a large sheet of paper such as newsprint, 12" x 18" construction paper, or 11" x 17" copy paper. Direct attention to additional supplies such as paper, markers, scissors, and glue. Challenge the teams to compose articles and to create illustrations describing the prayer experiences contained in their assigned book.

Suggest an editorial on the importance of prayer, a classified ad containing the job description of a disciple as a person of prayer, a map of the area in which Jesus and the disciples ministered, or a pictorial essay on one of Jesus' teachings on prayer. After pictures are drawn, stories are written, or activities are completed, the layout should be arranged in an attractive format and attached to the newspaper sheet.

Once the newspapers are compiled, ask each team to pass their reports to the group to their right. Allow time for the students to review each other's work. Continue passing projects until each group has read all five newspapers. Conclude by asking individuals to identify the differences and the similarities contained in each of the accounts.

An alternative to this would be to have each group read their newspaper to the class, and show the graphics and pictures. When all the newspapers have been displayed to the group, have a discussion about the differences and similarities in each.

14 Works of Mercy

GOAL

To review the fourteen works of mercy—the seven corporal and seven spiritual guides for showing love for God, self, and others—and to construct a "prayer prompter" as a reminder to put the words into action.

GATHER

- Construction paper, 12" x 18"
- Pens
- Rulers
- Scissors
- Pattern for prayer prompter (see page 38)

In advance:

- Make a prayer prompter (see directions in Guide section).
- Cut construction paper into 41/2" x 12" pieces, one per person.
- Cut 4" x 2" pieces of construction paper, seven per person.
- Prepare a poster listing the seven corporal works of mercy:
  - *Feed the hungry.*
  - *Give drink to the thirsty.*
  - *Clothe the naked.*
  - *Visit the imprisoned.*
  - *Shelter the homeless.*
  - *Visit the sick.*
  - *Bury the dead.*
- Prepare a poster listing the seven spiritual works of mercy:
  - *Help the sinner.*
  - *Teach the ignorant*
  - *Counsel the doubtful.*
  - *Comfort the sorrowful.*
  - *Bear wrongs patiently.*
  - *Forgive injuries.*
  - *Pray for the living and the dead.*

GUIDE

Fourteen is a number associated with a special day in February. Ask the participants to name the holiday. Valentine's Day is the answer! Valentine's Day, February 14, focuses on a specific theme. Invite the group to name the topic highlighted on Valentine's Day. This time, the answer is love.

Tell the learners that there are fourteen guides for living, also connected to the theme of love, that Christians have observed for hundreds of years. Invite someone to name the fourteen precepts known as the "works of mercy." The fourteen works of mercy are divided into two groups: seven corporal works, and seven spiritual works. Explain to students that the word "corporal" means "of the body," while the word "spiritual" refers to "things of the spirit, or of the soul."

Display the two lists that you have written up on posterboard, and review the fourteen works of mercy. Ask the group to name ways that the two lists are alike and ways that they are different. (Both sets of seven works are based on showing love for God, self, and others. In general, the spiritual works are of a personal nature, while the corporal works involve public acts.) Note that all fourteen works of mercy are intended to bring about God's Kingdom. Compare and contrast the two lists until the learners run out of ideas.

Extend the activity by discussing specific examples of ways to live the works of mercy. Remind the learners that these fourteen directives must be woven into our lives and carried out everyday, not just when we are reminded of them. The fourteen works of mercy challenge us to put love into action. We should try to serve God, to worship, to praise, and to pray, seven days a week.

Invite the group to make prayer prompters as a way to help them remember to observe the works of mercy. Show an example of a completed prayer prompter, and demonstrate the process for constructing this teaching tool. Take one 4 1/2" x 12" piece of construction paper. Fold the paper heightwise into thirds, with four inches in each section. Using the pattern provided, cut two vertical slits in the center section of the strip. The slits should be 2 1/4" long and 3" apart. Fold the paper on the dotted lines, as indicated on the pattern. The prayer prompter should now be triangular shaped. Fold a 1/4" tab on one of the short ends, then glue the tab in place at the bottom of the opposite end.

Now take seven pieces of 4" x 2" paper. Holding the paper horizontally, write one day of the week, Sunday through Saturday, in the left-hand corner of each piece. Next, write one of the corporal works of mercy on the right side of the strip. (It will be helpful to write the word "corporal" or to print the letters "CW" somewhere on this side of the strip.)

Turn the construction paper pieces over and repeat the process, only this time write the days of the week on the left side and print one of the spiritual works of mercy on the right side of each paper. (Include the word "spiritual" or the letters "SW.") Insert the seven slips in order, with Sunday at the top, into the center section of the prompter.

Distribute the supplies and guide the group as they construct their own prayer prompters. Once the projects are completed, provide instructions for using the teaching tool. On Sunday, pray the first prayer related to the corporal works of mercy. Ask for God's guidance in sharing love in this specific situation.

Remove the slip, turn it over, and place it on the bottom of the prayer prompter. It may be necessary to slide the remaining six strips to the top. Pray the second idea on Monday, now at the top, and continue in this manner every day of the week. At the end of seven days, the first strip, Sunday, will be on top of the prompter, and the seven spiritual works of mercy will be facing forward. At this point, repeat the prayer process during the week.

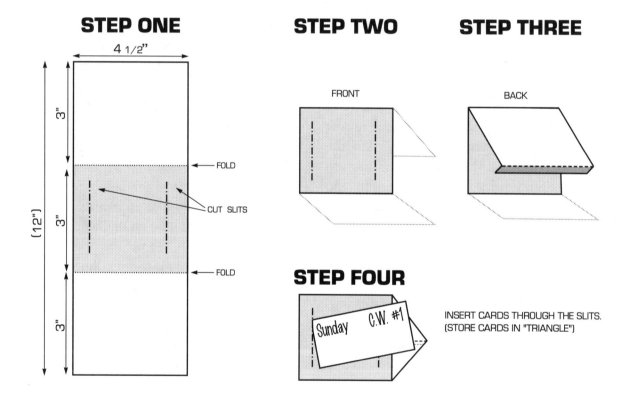

STEP ONE

4 1/2"

3"

(12")

3"

FOLD

CUT SLITS

3"

FOLD

STEP TWO

FRONT

STEP THREE

BACK

STEP FOUR

Sunday C.W. #1

INSERT CARDS THROUGH THE SLITS.
(STORE CARDS IN "TRIANGLE")

15 Stations of the Cross

GOAL

To illustrate the Stations of the Cross with cartoon-like panels, and to better understand the relevance of this traditional prayer in today's world.

GATHER

- Newsprint sheets, white construction paper, or cardboard cartons (15 pieces)
- Markers
- Old magazines and newspapers
- Glue
- Scissors
- Masking tape

GUIDE

The Stations of the Cross is a prayer that has been an enduring source of inspiration for Christians since the Middle Ages. Of late, however, this beautiful and meaningful devotional has been practiced less and less by young people who find it difficult to make an appropriate application of Jesus' sufferings to the world today and to their own daily lives.

This learning activity is intended to bridge the gap between youthful experience and mature meditation. A fifteenth station, the resurrection, has been added by many Christians, since the prayer is meaningless unless the living Christ is kept in mind.

Ask the group to name the fifteen parts to the Stations of the Cross. Help the learners by encouraging them to think about the things that could have happened as Jesus walked to Calvary. Don't be concerned with right or wrong answers or any particular order at this time.

Allow the students to talk through the possible events. For example, Jesus met people on the way and stopped to talk with them; Jesus got tired and thirsty; He was given a cross to carry; Jesus may have been sad, and so on. Write the group's ideas on newsprint. Allow time for all ideas. Once the participants have exhausted the possibilities for identifying the stations, check to see how many stations the students actually named in their brainstorming.

Invite the students to think about ways in which the fifteen Stations of the Cross relate to events in today's world.

Brainstorm how each station parallels a contemporary situation. For example, "Jesus is condemned to death" might remind the group of starving children in the Third World, or, "Jesus falls" may suggest a memory of an elderly person alone and frightened, or "Jesus dies" could prompt stories of gang violence. Tell the group that they will have the opportunity to use these ideas to create cartoons depicting the Stations of the Cross as they relate to everyday life.

The following meditation could be used before creating the cartoons to give the learners ideas for their projects.

1. *Jesus is Condemned to Death*

There are many people on death row, Lord. Many of our people are homeless, they live in the street. We look down on them.

Condemned, Lord! Who gave us that right? To stand above another creature, to look down, to judge. How powerful we feel...how unlike you we are.

2. *Jesus Takes Up his Cross*

The elderly are forgotten, Lord. People are dying everywhere from AIDS. Too many crosses.

Yet you are more powerful than all the crosses in the world. Love makes our crosses lighter.

3. *Jesus Falls the First Time*

The youth of our world are tempted to give in to drugs and sexual pressures. People are put down and called names.

It hurts to fall and be broken, Lord. Drained of all your dignity...I thought you always wanted me to stand straight! Help me fit my idea of "straight" to yours, Lord.

4. *Jesus Meets his Mother*

These are good people God, giving and helping those who are hurting. Words can be a comfort for those in pain. Mother and son have given completely.

Love makes you feel a real part of another. You feel their pain and their joys, and they feel yours.

5. *Simon Helps Jesus Carry the Cross*

Soup kitchens, shelters for the homeless, clothing centers, hospice care, a good friend...are all cross-carrying helpers, Lord. People reaching out, people caring enough to give. When there are two to carry the cross it seems lighter.

We don't each have a separate cross, Lord. Teach us to help one another.

6. *Veronica Helps Jesus*

Lord, thank you for our families and friends, they help to wipe the tears. They stop and look into our eyes and take the time to care and love. It takes courage to look into the face of another, to help.

7. *Jesus Falls Again*

Broken again!

8. *Jesus Meets the Women*

Thank you, God, for the feminine influence. For mothers and grandmothers, sisters and daughters. They have borne us, and raised us, and given us love.

9. *Jesus Falls a Third Time*

Three times, Lord! No person could stand this...straight, Lord! Killing and cheating, lying and hating. Do you mean supernaturally straight, with your grace? Is *that* how we are to stand? Not as others see, but as you see.

10. Jesus is Stripped of his Clothes

They have nothing, Lord. They are poor and destitute. Freedom is gone. Everything I think belongs to me has been ripped off. Sometimes, being stripped is to be free, free from things, free to love deeply.

11. Jesus Is Crucified

Only pure love can be rooted this deep, deeper than nails could place it. There is no greater love, than to die for a friend.

12. Jesus Dies

All human life must come to an end; we must all face death. May we look at the end of life as a gift, a passage that brings us to you, our God.

13. Jesus is Taken Down from the Cross

To help another person out, to wipe a tear, give a smile…these are the ways we learn to love as you did. When we become like you we allow ourself to be moved by another.

14. Jesus Is Buried

The tomb wasn't even Jesus' own. Help us understand your life, so that we, too, can rise.

15. Jesus Rises from the Dead

A newborn baby…flowers in spring…two people deeply in love with each other…a mother or father with their child…the break of dawn; you *are* alive! You have come back and are with us always!

Organize the learners into fifteen groups and assign one station to each team. Distribute a sheet of newsprint, a piece of white construction paper, or a cardboard carton to each group. Provide markers and direct the students to print the name of their assigned station on the piece of paper or carton. Suggest that each group draw several, possibly four, frames for their cartoon strip. (These "cartoons" should not be funny; rather, using a cartoon style of drawing.) If boxes are used, one frame could be created on each side of a carton.

Provide magazines, newspapers, scissors, and glue. Tell the participants to use these materials to illustrate the scenes they wish to depict. Pictures and words may be cut from magazines and newspapers and attached to the frames, and words and images can be drawn on the cartoon strips, as well. Guide the group as they work on their projects.

Once the activity is completed and clean-up has taken place, display the cartoon strips, in order, around the room. Tape newsprint or construction paper sheets to the walls, or line up the cartons. Ask the group to share their strips and to talk about what they learned by participating in a project related to this traditional prayer.

16 Old Testament Prophets

GOAL

To survey the prayers of the Old Testament prophets and use selected verses to construct a ribbon banner, thereby gaining a better understanding of God.

GATHER

- Bibles
- Paper and pencils
- Newsprint
- Masking tape
- Several permanent black markers
- Ribbon, 16 pieces of various colors, 1" wide and cut into 1 yard strips
- 20" long wooden dowel

GUIDE

A prophet is a person who responds to God's call, even in the face of great difficulties. Prophets keep the covenant and do God's loving will. All people are invited by God to be prophets in the world.

A prophet does not tell the future but is called by God to speak out and to remind people how God wants them to live today. A prophet proclaims faithfulness to God in word and action. A prophet encourages people to obey God's law and to act justly. The prophets had much to say about how to live life in tenderness, in justice, and in close union with God.

The prophetic books of the Old Testament reflect the human experiences of suffering, sadness, and discouragement.

In the history of the Hebrew people, their greatest spiritual growth took place during their lowest and most discouraging times. Use this activity to offer participants a vision of hope to help them cope with the disappointments and discouragements they may experience in their own lives. Challenge the learners to live out the message of the prophets, and to heed their words of prayer.

Organize the class into sixteen pairs or small groups. Distribute Bibles, paper, and pencils, and assign each group one of the sixteen prophetic books of the Old Testament. These are: Isaiah, Jeremiah, Ezekiel, Zephaniah, Daniel, Hosea, Joel, Amos, Obadiah, Jonah,

Micah, Nahum, Habakkuk, Haggai, Zechariah, and Malachi.

Invite the groups to skim through their assigned book. Encourage the learners to write down prayers, statements about prayer, and prophetic advice on how people should live their lives.

After the teams have collected several statements, regather the large group. Ask each cluster to read two or three passages from their prophetic book and invite the class to select one of the references to be used to create a ribbon banner. Write the chosen verse on a piece of newsprint. Continue this process until all groups have had a turn to report. The following passages may be used as examples, if additional ideas are needed.

Isaiah 12:1

On that day, in prayer you will say: "I give you thanks, O Lord; though you have been angry with me, your anger has abated, and you have consoled me."

Jeremiah 31:33

I will place my law within them, and write it upon their hearts; I will be their God, and they shall be my people.

Ezekiel 37:14

I will put my spirit in you that you may have life, and I will settle you upon your land; thus you shall know that I am the Lord. I promised, and I will do it, says the Lord.

Daniel 2:23

To you O God of my fathers, I pray in thanksgiving, because you have given me wisdom and strength. For it is love that I desire, not sacrifice, and knowledge of God rather than holocausts.

Joel 2:27

Remember always, I am the Lord your God, and there is no other; my people shall never more be put to shame.

Amos 6:1

Woe to the complacent and overconfident.

Obadiah 1:15

As you have done, so shall it be done to you.

Jonah 2:3

For out of my prayer I called to you Lord, and you answered me; from my distress I cried for help, and you heard my voice.

Micah 6:8

The Lord your God asks only this: Only to do right, to love goodness, and to walk humbly with your God.

Nahum 1:7

The Lord is good, a refuge on the day of distress; he takes care of those who have recourse to him.

Habakkuk 3:19

God, my Lord, is my strength; he makes my feet swift as those of hinds and enables me to go upon the heights.

Zephaniah 2:3

Seek the Lord, all you humble of the earth, seek justice, seek humility.

Haggai 1:13

I am with you, says the Lord.

Zechariah 10:1

Pray to the Lord for your needs. For he sends the pouring rain in the spring season!

Malachi 2:10

Have we not all one Father? Has not one God created us? Why then do we break faith with each other, violating the covenant?

Once sixteen passages have been collected and written down on the newsprint, distribute the ribbon and markers, one set per group. Invite each group to print their selected verse, or a summary of it, on one side of the ribbon. Tell the teams to print the name of the prophet, as well as the chapter and verse number for their passage on the back of the ribbon. For example:

Front: Pray to the Lord for your needs.
Back: Zechariah 10:1

Collect the ribbons as they are completed, and glue or staple the tops around a long dowel rod. Be sure the verses all face the same direction. Display the ribbon banner for all to see.

Invite the group to share what they learned from the prophetic messages and how these Old Testament words relate to their own lives today. Talk together about ways young people can speak out against injustice to be prophetic. Ask questions like: Why does being a prophet take courage? Do you believe that you have been chosen by God to do something that only you can do? How can you be a prophet of hope, like Ezekiel, during hard times in your family?

In closing, pray the following verses from Jeremiah 1:5,9 with the group:

I chose you before I gave you life, and before you were born I selected you to be a prophet to the nations. Listen, I place my words in your mouth.

FRONT   **BACK**

Pray to the Lord for your needs.

Zechariah 10:1

17 Saint Patrick's Prayers

GOAL

To review the prayers of Saint Patrick, whose feast day is celebrated March 17, then have participants use writing and movement to offer their own prayers to God.

GATHER

- Historical and biographical information about Saint Patrick
- Paper and pencils
- Candles and matches
- Tape or CD player, and tape or CD of gentle background music

GUIDE

Prayer is important to our lives as Christians. And prayer was especially important to the saint whose feast day is celebrated on March 17. Ask the group to name this person: Saint Patrick. Share the story of Saint Patrick with the students, telling of his deep faith and his work to bring the Gospel to the people of Ireland. Explain that very little is known about Saint Patrick's early life. As a boy of fourteen, Patrick was carried off by raiders and taken to Ireland as a slave. In his captivity, Patrick turned to God.

Read the group some of the writings of Patrick to help illustrate his life of prayer and his commitment to God. In his writings Saint Patrick tells us:

The love of God and his mercy grew in me more and more, as did the faith, and my soul was roused, so that in a single day, I have said as many as a hundred

prayers and in the nights nearly the same.

Prayer was Patrick's life. He would often go to distant places to speak with God. One of the best known places where Patrick spent time in prayer and fasting was Croagh Patrick, or "Saint Patrick's mountain." In fact, Patrick said: *I prayed in the woods, in the fields, and on the mountain, even before dawn.*

Patrick gave until he had no more to give, and was happy to see himself poor with Jesus. He knew that poverty and prayer would bring him closer to God. One reason for Patrick's great holiness was his deep humility. He wrote a book called the "Confessions," in which he speaks about his relationship with God.

I give unceasing thanks to my God, who kept me faithful in the day of my testing. Today I can offer him sacrifice with confidence, giving myself as a living sacrifice to Christ, who kept me safe through all my trials.

God showed me how to have faith forever, as one who is never to be doubted. God answered my prayer in such a way that, I might be bold enough to take up so holy and wonderful a task, and imitate in some way those whom Jesus has so long ago foretold as heralds of his Gospel.

Ask the students if prayer is important in their lives. How do they pray? When do they pray? Where do they pray? How do they know that God hears their prayers? How do they listen to God speaking to them? Share reactions to these questions.

Continue the discussion by asking the group to share their feelings on statements such as: How do you live the Gospel? What idols do you have in your own life? Who are the people walking with you and showing you the way? Give the students an opportunity to speak freely of their own experiences in relation to the experiences of Saint Patrick.

When the discussion winds down, offer a time of silence for personal reflection. Distribute paper and pencils, and give the participants an opportunity to share their own life experiences by writing prayers to God. Light the candle and play soft music in the background.

An Irish Blessing

As a way to celebrate the life and work of Saint Patrick, conclude by reciting a traditional Irish blessing and interpreting it with gestures and sign language. Read the prayer to the group:

May the road rise to meet you.
May the wind be always at your back.
May the sun shine warm upon your face,
The rain fall soft upon your fields.

And, until we meet again,
May God hold you in the palm of his hand.

Interpret each word with a gesture and ask the group to repeat the action:

*May…*Extend hands in front of body, palms up.

*The road…*Move hands in front of body in zigzag motion.

*Rise…*Lift hands over head.

*To…*Direct the right index finger toward, and then touch, the left index fingertip which is pointing up.

*Meet…*Bring both hands together from the sides so the palms meet, fingers bent in and thumb and index finger pointing out.

*You…*Point one index finger out.

*May…*Extend hands in front of body.

*The wind…*Hold the hands high, palms together, the left slightly lower than the right; move them towards the left in several sweeping motions.

*Be…*Place the tip of the index finger at the mouth; move it forward, still upright.

*Always…*Make a clockwise circle in front of the body with the index finger, palm facing up.

*At…*Hold the left hand in front of the body, palm out. Strike the back of the left hand with the tips of the right hand, both hands pointing upward.

*Your…*Face the right palm out, directing it forward.

*Back…*Touch back with right hand crossing over left shoulder.

*May…*Extend hands in front of body.

*The sun…*Draw a clockwise circle in the air.

*Shine…*Open palms facing each other with tips pointing up. Wiggle fingers.

*Warm…*Place the right fist in front of the mouth, palm in, and open the hand gradually as it moves slightly up and out.

Upon...Point up with right index finger.

Your...Face the palm out and forward.

Face...Using the right index finger, trace a circle in front of the face.

The rain...Let both curved hands drop down several times in short, quick motions.

Fall...Form a "V" with two fingers of the right hand and place it in a standing position on the left palm; let the "V" fall, palm down, into the left hand.

Soft...Point open hands upward, then draw them down, fingers together.

Upon...Point up with the right index finger.

Your...Face the palm out and forward.

Fields...Rub the fingertips of both hands with the thumb as if feeling soil; make a counterclockwise circle with the right open hand, palm down.

And...Place the right hand in front of body, fingers spread apart and point left. Draw the hand to the right, closing the tips.

Until...Direct the right index finger in a forward arc and touch the left index finger, which is pointing up.

We...Place the index finger at the right shoulder and circle it forward and around until it touches the left shoulder.

Meet...Bring both hands together from the sides so the palms meet, fingers bend in, and thumb and index finger point out.

Again...The right curved hand faces up, then turns and moves to the left so that the fingertips touch the left palm which is pointing forward with the palm facing right. Repeat action several times.

May...Extend hands in front of body.

God...Point the right index finger forward in front of you, draw it up and back down, opening the palm which is facing left.

Hold...Both open hands, palms up, move from right to left in front of body.

You...Point one index finger out.

In...Place the closed fingertips of the right hand into the left half-circled hand.

The palm...Point to left palm with right index finger.

Of his...Point the right index finger forward in front of you, draw it up and back down, opening the palm which is facing left.

Hand...Stroke the back of the left hand with the right hand and reverse the action.

seventeen

18 The Pharisee & the Publican

GOAL

To review the parable of the "Pharisee and the Publican," found in Luke 18:9–14, then to make and use puppets to learn the proper attitude for prayer.

GATHER

- Bibles
- Paper tubes, any size
- Felt and fabric scraps
- Yarn or fake fur
- Scissors
- Glue
- Craft sticks or dowel rods

GUIDE

In the Gospel of Luke, Jesus not only teaches his disciples a pattern for prayer (the Lord's Prayer, found in chapter 11:1–4), he also provides his followers with instructions for the proper attitude for prayer. In Luke 18:9–14, the passage commonly known as "The Parable of the Pharisee and the Publican (tax collector)," Jesus instructs us to pray honestly and humbly. He also reminds us to pray sincerely, like the tax collector, and not self-righteously, like the Pharisee.

Look up Luke 18:9–14 in a Bible and read the verses to the students. Offer various translations of God's Word, and invite the participants to compare the passage in different versions. Tell the group that they will make puppets from

paper tubes and that they will write a script or improvise actions to tell the story of the Pharisee and the publican.

Use paper towel tubes or toilet paper rolls for average-sized puppets, or try wrapping paper tubes or carpet rolls for giant characters. Form the puppet face by cutting a piece of felt and gluing it to the top one-third of the cardboard. Make facial features from felt scraps and glue them in place. Attach yarn or fake fur to the top of the tube for hair.

Glue a piece of felt around the remainder of the tube to serve as the undergarment. Layers of fabric in contrasting or complementary colors can be added as overgarments. Make arms from strips of cloth or felt and glue them to the sides of the tube. Apply a craft stick to the inside back of the tube to serve as the rod by which the puppet is operated.

If felt is not available, use construction paper instead. The facial features may be drawn on with marker. Substitute tissue paper for fabric to form the outer garments.

When the puppets have been made, write a puppet show to act out the Luke 18:9–14 passage. The story needs to have a beginning, a middle, and an end. These can also be called Acts I, II, and III. Start by deciding the action that takes place in each scene. Write short, simple dialogue between the characters. In Act One, the beginning, establish the time and place. Introduce the main characters and their relationship to each other. Establish the conflict.

During Act Two, the middle, list the series of events that move toward the climax, or confrontation, of the conflict. In the end, Act Three, resolve the conflict in a believable way. Determine the props and scenery that will be needed to enhance the story. Act out the story, using the tube puppet characters.

Since the parable of the Pharisee and the publican is familiar to most people, you can also use the tube puppets to improvise the Bible passage. (To improvise means to compose and to perform without preparation.) Here there is no specific script, and no right or wrong way to tell the story. Read or review the account found in Luke 18:9–14 and instruct the puppeteers to portray the action, with or without words. Allow the participants to take turns playing various parts.

Conclude the session with the prayer of a publican rather than a prayer of a Pharisee; that is, with an honest, humble request for God's help in sustaining a proper attitude of prayer. *(Turn the page for an illustrated guide to making a tube puppet.)*

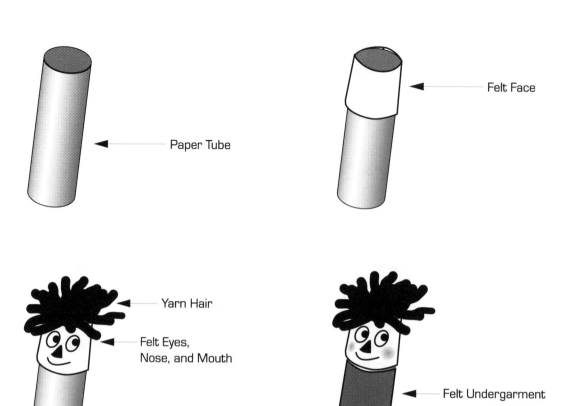

Paper Tube

Felt Face

Yarn Hair

Felt Eyes,
Nose, and Mouth

Felt Undergarment

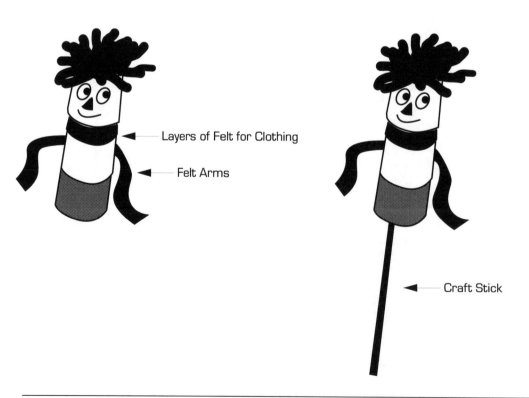

Layers of Felt for Clothing

Felt Arms

Craft Stick

19 The Gospels

GOAL

To study the four Gospels—Matthew, Mark, Luke, and John—and review nineteen passages related to Jesus' teachings on prayer.

GATHER

- Bibles (one per person)
- Paper
- Pencils

GUIDE

Ask the participants to name the four Gospels—Matthew, Mark, Luke, and John. Challenge the group to guess what the number nineteen has to do with these books. If no one offers the correct answer, state that there are nineteen letters in the words Matthew, Mark, Luke, and John.

Count the letters together. Invite the participants to recall some of their favorite stories from the Gospels. Distribute Bibles, and encourage the learners to look up various texts. Once the students have had an opportunity to share their selections, ask the group to talk about Jesus' teachings on prayer. What examples and instructions are recorded in these New Testament books? Allow time for discussion.

Hand out paper and pencils. Explain that the group will search the first four books of the New Testament to study nineteen passages related to the theme of prayer.

The Gospel of John

Ask the students to look up five passages in their Bibles. Invite discussion and sharing on the message of each text.

> John 10:10
> John 14:6
> John 15:1–10
> John 13:1–15
> John 2:13–22

Explain that one of the most important insights of John's Gospel is that John invites all people to live life to the fullest. Stress that God not only desires to give fullness of life but also helps us to achieve this abundant life. Invite the participants to sit quietly for a minute or two. Ask them to read the Scripture texts again, silently and meditatively. Pause for a moment or two of reflection.

Mark's Gospel

Invite the students to close their eyes for a moment. Ask them to "just be" in God's presence. Tell the group that they will use Mark's Gospel to help them pray over the stories of Jesus' last days on earth. Have the participants look up the following passages in their Bibles. Ask them to write down the main message of each text. Allow time for work and sharing.

> Mark 14:22–26
> Mark 14:32–41
> Mark 15:16–20
> Mark 15:21–37
> Mark 16:1–19

Luke's Gospel

Encourage the students to find and to read five Scripture passages in the Gospel of Luke. Ask them to make note of how these texts speak of prayer and of the strength believers gain by having God in their lives.

> Luke 4:1–13
> Luke 9:18–22
> Luke 19:1–10
> Luke 24:13–35
> Luke 22:36–39

Matthew's Gospel

Invite the students to use the Gospel of Matthew to pray over important aspects of Jesus' life. Encourage students to share findings and to cite the importance of each passage for their own personal lives. Ask the students to write down the main point of each passage.

> Matthew 4:18–22
> Matthew 9:1–8
> Matthew 15:32–38
> Matthew 17:1–9

Once the Scripture study is completed, encourage the students to read a passage from one of the Gospels every night as a way of getting closer to Jesus through prayer.

20 Fingers & Toes

GOAL

To participate in a handprint/footprint banner painting project, and identify people who may be in need of prayer.

GATHER

- Chalkboard and chalk, or newsprint and markers
- Bedsheet, white (or cotton fabric)
- Masking or duct tape
- Tempera paint, variety of colors
- Dishpans
- Water
- Liquid soap
- Bath towels or paper towels
- Permanent markers

GUIDE

Prayer is an important part of daily life. Without God, life can be overwhelming, and seem impossible to deal with. Prayer is part of a friendship that exists between God and God's people. Lifting up mind and heart to God is one definition of prayer. Yet prayer, like poetry, is hard to define. With your class, write twenty definitions of prayer on the chalkboard or on a piece of newsprint. Here are some examples:

A hymn...

A love song...

Being in the company of the One who deeply loves you...

Telling God you're sorry...

Being dissolved into Someone greater than yourself...

A response for God's love...

Thanking God for God's gifts...

Asking God for something...

Communication with God.

Ask the participants to read the statements and to choose the one that seems closest to their own interpretation of prayer. Invite the students to share with the group why they chose a particular answer. Remind the group of the ACTS prayer step formula containing the four parts of prayer: adoration, contrition, thanksgiving, and supplication. Tell them that they will participate in a banner-making activity focusing on prayers of supplication.

Ask someone to define the word supplication. Explain that supplication means asking for or requesting something from God. When we pray, we communicate with a loving and caring God who wants nothing more than to give us what is best for our lives. Even when specific prayers don't seem to be granted, assure the group that God hears and answers every prayer. Invite the students to share prayer requests that they have made and answers that they have received. Examples could be getting an A on a test, making the team, and having a part in the school play.

Now ask if anyone has prayed a prayer of supplication on behalf of someone else. Of course, the answer will be yes. Examples might include praying that mom would get better when she is sick, asking God to be with a grandparent on a trip, and requesting help for dad during a big project.

Next, brainstorm a list of different groups of people who need to be remembered in prayer. Try to guide the suggestions to categories of people, rather than specific names. Challenge the students to come up with at least twenty different groups of people that need God's help. Write the students' responses on a sheet of newsprint. The following list could serve as a guide for the activity:

1. The hungry
2. The homeless
3. The unemployed
4. Parent(s)
5. Teenagers
6. Abused children
7. People in war
8. People with HIV/AIDS
9. People who are dying alone
10. People who are racist
11. Drug addicts

12. Kids who are in gangs
13. Kids who try to commit suicide
14. Teachers
15. Health care workers
16. Social workers
17. People who work for the rights and freedom of all people
18. Missionaries
19. People who teach the Gospel
20. All of us

Once a list has been compiled, invite the students to take part in a banner-making project as a way to remember people who need their prayers. Ask the group to guess why the number twenty has been used throughout this activity. Then ask the participants to name the way they learned to count, or the way they counted when they were very young—probably on their fingers and toes! Tell the group that they will make a unique banner by painting their fingers and toes on a large piece of fabric. Each finger and toe will represent a person who needs to be remembered in prayer.

Spread the bedsheet on the floor in the center of a large room. (Note that this project can be done outdoors, weather permitting, for less indoor cleanup.) Tape the corners and the sides of the cloth to the floor. Pour each color of tempera paint into a separate bowl or dishpan. Place only enough paint in the pans to cover palms of hands and bottoms of feet. Add a small amount of liquid soap to the paint to aid cleanup. Place the filled dishpans around the sides of the sheet.

Invite the banner makers to remove their shoes and socks. Instruct one or two participants at a time to choose a color, and carefully step into the bowl or dishpan containing it. Direct each person to slowly walk across the sheet. Be sure that the toes on each foot are imprinted on the fabric. Provide bath towels or wet paper towels at the end of the walk and assist with cleanup. Continue this procedure until everyone has had a turn.

Next, add handprints to the banner by instructing one or two pupils at a time to choose a color of paint and to carefully place both hands into the dishpan containing it. Direct each person to press his or her hands onto the fabric, making sure that each finger forms a clear print. Provide cleanup assistance. As the banner is being created remind the students that there are as many people who need prayers of supplication as there are fingers and toes on the banner. Note that when one color touches another, a change takes place. Comment that when we pray for Jesus to touch people's lives, changes can take place too.

Once all of the participants have had a opportunity to add hand- and footprints to the banner, set the piece aside to dry. Refer to the brainstormed list, and ask the class to pick twenty groups of people to include on the banner—one representing each finger and each toe. When the banner is completely dry, invite the students to write the twenty words around or in twenty different hand- or footprints. Provide permanent markers for this purpose.

Hang the completed project in a prominent location for all to see. In closing, read slowly and thoughtfully the following paraphrase from the first letter of John to the Christian community.

Beloved,
   let us love one another
   because love is of God;
   everyone who loves
   is begotten of God
   and has knowledge of God.
The person without love
   has known nothing of God,
   for God is love.
God's love was revealed
   in our midst in this way:
God sent Jesus, the Son, into the world
   that we might have life
   through him.
Love, then, consists in this:
   not that we have loved God,
   but that God has loved us
   and has sent Jesus
   as an offering for our sins.
Beloved, if God has loved us so,
   we must have the same love
   for one another.
No one has ever seen God.
Yet if we love one another
   God dwells in us,
   and God's love is brought
   to perfection in us.
We have come to know
   and to believe in the love
   God has for us.
God is love,
   any one who abides in love
   abides in God,
   and God in them.

               1 John 4:7–16

Conclude by offering a prayer for the twenty groups named on the hand- and footprint banner. Invite the students to count them on fingers and toes while the prayer is being recited.

Resources

Caprio, Betsy. *Experiments In Prayer.* Notre Dame, IN: Ave Maria Press, 1973.

Chesto, Kathleen O. *Family Prayer for Family Times: Traditions, Celebrations, and Rituals.* Mystic, CT: Twenty-Third Pub7lications, 1995.

Costello, Gwen. *Prayer Services for Young Adolescents.* Mystic, CT: Twenty-Third Publications, 1994.

Cronin, Gaynell Bordes. *Holy Days and Holidays: Prayer Celebrations With Children* (2 volumes). San Francisco: Harper & Row, 1985, 1988.

Glavich, Kathleen. *Leading Students Into Prayer.* Mystic, CT: Twenty-Third Publications, 1993.

Jessie, Karen. *Praying With Children Grades 4-6.* Villa Maria, PA: The Center For Learning, 1986.

Jones, Timothy and Jill Zook-Jones. *Prayer: Discovering What Scripture Says.* Wheaton, IL: Harold Shaw Publishers, 1993.

Manternach, Janaan with Carl J. Pfeifer. *And The Children Pray.* Notre Dame, IN: Ave Maria Press, 1989.

Mathson, Patricia. *Pray & Play: 28 Prayer Services and Activities for Children In K Through Sixth Grade.* Notre Dame, IN: Ave Maria Press, 1989.

Rezy, Carol. *Liturgies for Little Ones: 38 Celebrations for Grades One to Three.* Notre Dame, IN: Ave Maria Press, 1978.

Schreiber, Gayle. *Prayers Services for Young Children: 30 Ten Minute Celebrations.* Mystic, CT: Twenty-Third Publications, 1993.

Smith, Judy Gattis. *Teaching Children About Prayer.* Prescott, AZ: Educational Ministries, 1988.

Wezeman, Phyllis Vos and Anna L. Liechty. *Hymn Stories for Children: The Lord's Prayer.* Grand Rapids, MI: Kregel Publications, 1996.

Of Related Interest...

20 More Prayer Lessons for Children
Phyllis Vos Wezeman and Jude Dennis Fournier
From the authors who wrote the original *20 Prayer Lessons for Children*, here are 20 more fun and faith-filled ways to teach children to pray. Each practical lesson is centered around an activity designed to bring out a particular prayer theme.

ISBN: 0-89622-736-7, 64 pp, $9.95

Children, Imagination and Prayer
Creative Techniques for Middle Grade Students
Pat Egan Dexter
Using techniques that combine imagination, relaxation, and guided imagery, the author gives step-by-step directions for bringing students to a new and meditative experience of prayer, referred to as "picture prayer." Part One shows teachers how to help students understand why and how picture prayer works. Part Two offers ten step-by-step exercises on various themes which guide students into picture prayer. Great help for busy teachers and parents.

ISBN: 0-89622-565-8, 80 pp, $7.95

25 Guided Prayer Services for Middle Graders
Pat Egan Dexter
This creative, user-friendly prayer service book connects the real-life experiences of children with the words of Scripture. Each service highlights one of the many gifts children have received from God: gifts of nature, talents, virtues, etc. The services begin with Scripture readings focusing on each topic, followed by a hands-on activity and a guided meditation. A closing prayer involving all the children in the group brings each service to an end.

ISBN: 0-89622-688-3, 88 pp, $12.95

Prayer Services for Young Adolescents
Gwen Costello
Common concerns of 10-14 year-olds such as: peer pressure, clothes, smoking, drugs, faith, prayer, alcohol, profanity, sex and sexuality, are addressed through group and private prayer and Scripture reflections. Particularly appealing is the guided meditation in each service.

ISBN: 0-89622-597-6, 80 pp, $9.95

Leading Students Into Prayer
Ideas and Suggestions from A to Z
Mary Kathleen Glavich, S.N.D.
The author explores the varied forms that prayer can take for children: personal and communal, vocal and mental, liturgical, Scripture-based, centering, and traditional. Any teacher with a personal copy of this treasure-store of prayer activities and techniques will have many exciting ideas to incorporate into religion lessons, as well as for personal inspiration and practice.

ISBN: 0-89622-549-6, 160 pp, $14.95

 TWENTY-THIRD PUBLICATIONS
P.O. Box 180 • Mystic, CT 06355
1-800-321-0411
E-Mail:ttpubs@aol.com